UNLOCK *your* INNER MAGIC

Practical Intuition for Everyday Life

CALLIE CLAIRE, MA, NLP

Unlock Your Inner Magic:
Practical Intuition for Everyday Life

TABLE OF CONTENTS

I have nothing but amazing things to say about my time with Callie Claire, a sensitive and insightful life coach and spiritual healer. She has given me an incredibly personalized toolbox and helped me to see with new perspective just where to put those tools to work. She brings such a diverse set of abilities to the table -- she is perceptive in practical ways, she is a gifted intuitive, and she is also remarkably in tune with her clients' own personal process and ability to process the often life changing information she brings. She is down to earth and kind, but doesn't hesitate to bring tough love. It is ever-evident in a session that she has your highest good in mind - even if it is you yourself who is standing in your own way. From a practical standpoint, Callie is the consummate professional. – Jill Summers

Mind-blowing! Incredible! Remarkable! Life Changing! I have so much admiration for Callie and everything she's helped me through. We've been connected since the day we met.
– Jamie Kidd

Callie is a light of lights, an outlier. – Frank Byrum

Callie and I had an INSTANT connection. Her beautiful, positive soul always has a person's highest and best interest at heart. She has a true gift, she willing shares. – Greta Stallings

Perfectly enlightening! -Katharine Bailey

Callie, a true angel in every sense-compassionate, thoughtful, and blessed with an extraordinary ability. – Rupa Chatterjee

Personal Note:

Unlock Your Intuition is designed for those ready to trust their inner voice and embrace the power of their intuition. Whether you're experiencing a spiritual awakening, seeking closure after a loss, or looking to develop your psychic and healing abilities, this book provides a proven and practical formula to guide you.

In fact, it holds ***a powerful secret*** that is in plain sight, a type of memory retrieval that each of us uses multiple times a day. This resource is a natural method of unlocking your inner wisdom. Once you understand the timeless power this underlying spiritual communication tool offers you, that "*A-Ha!*" feeling will continue to empower you every blessed day of your life.

With hands-on exercises, personal stories, and expert insights, <u>I've done the work for you</u> by pulling together the most effective tools and practices into one clear, accessible guide.

This work is powerful. It is deeply meaningful to me. The path to the fruition of your innate abilities is different for everyone. As a child hostage survivor who was just a kid who loved Sherlock Holmes and Joan Aiken ghost stories, who was fascinated by all the stories of the *Titanic*- maybe it was inevitable that this Calling would become a driving force in my life. And a "calling" is what this Gift is… It is personal.

This healing work bridges neuroscience and energy healing. It involves a deep empathy and compassion that offers alternative healing pathways that are akin to grief and trauma coaching and to life purpose empowerment <u>that are parallel to traditional</u>

psychological methods. In other words, please don't rely on me or any other alternative healing practitioner for medical or psychological advice.

Now, as a psychic intuitive who was on TV for many years, I can tell you that my career path is quite different. As a multi-award-winning interior designer, Inc 5000, and as an award-winning painter I have learned the benefits of marrying the intuitive and the practical.

We are spiritual beings leading a human life. My soul-self cannot watch the kids in the pool, for want of a better analogy. My spirit must be grounded in everyday living.

When my babies were small, my mind needed a challenge. So, after years of writing and having manuscripts stolen (really…) I chose to pursue a Masters degree in World War II Military History because I wanted to breathe life in my Pappy's stories, and to ensure my research capabilities were top notch- fast forward I graduated with a 4.0GPA and nonfiction narrative manuscripts focusing on harrowing, until now forgotten stories of the power of women behind-the-scenes have been endorsed for publication at prestigious university presses. War is the story of life, death and rebirth in a microcosm.

The spirit of resilience for these people (many of whom I am privileged to know) is a touchstone of inspiration for me. Certainly, my intuition- my daily bread- was a huge factor in being able to seek out the untold stories and perspectives that inform my work.

Outstanding intuition, for me, is a great responsibility. As a successful creative entrepreneur, whose livelihood is built upon my ability to visualize interiors and then flawlessly install them for a demanding C-Suite clientele it may appear to be a small leap from visualization to full blown evidential mediumship and psychic ability. It is not.

It is a duty-driven Gift that is real and precious to me. It is a large facet of my personality, my life. I infuse this healing work with integrity. It melds EQ + IQ, which is why I coined the title The Intuitive Academic.

The road to realizing my psychic abilities was rocky. It was scary. Living in a 175-year-old house- alone- only exacerbated the feelings of disruption. Dealing with cranky other energies (I refrain from using the "p---------t" word or the "d-----n" word, even in jest) was not easy. BUT!

What I had to learn, what I was forced to learn, was that the same boundaries intrusive spirits demanded I engage are the same boundaries I needed to learn for daily life. Period. Your boundaries are flexible, energetic flows of emotion- or energy in motion- and this work will uplevel your life in every way.

You'll learn how to build confidence in your intuitive gifts, interpret dreams, connect with spirit guides, and heal emotional wounds. Whether you're new to spiritual development or have experience, this book offers practical strategies to help you heal, grow, and unlock the full potential of your intuition. If you're looking for clarity, guidance, and empowerment on your journey, *Unlock Your Intuition* will give you the tools you need to succeed.

Because as I gained confidence, as I met my peers, others commented on the big, loving group of souls that stewarded my path. One close friend and business mentor says that "I exude joy"- that is a choice. It is a choice embedded in a deep, spiritual faith that my loved ones are watching over me, and it gives me hope. Deep, abiding hope. An unshakeable faith in the goodness of the world. And as equally as I am in the world of healing, as equally as I am in the world of practical magic making.

INTRODUCTION:
Trusting the Whispers of Your Soul

In a world full of noise, learning to trust the whispers of your intuition can feel like trying to hear a soft melody in the middle of a storm. Yet, those whispers—those subtle nudges, gut feelings, and seemingly random thoughts—are your most reliable guide. They are the quiet compass that leads you through life's uncertainties, helping you make decisions that align with your highest good.

My own journey with intuition wasn't something I planned. In fact, like many of you, I was swept into it by forces far beyond my control. I'll never forget the day my intuition peaked—a moment born out of sheer survival when I experienced the trauma of gun violence as a child. In that instant, everything around me slowed down, and my senses became heightened in a way I'd never felt before. It was as though a door had been opened to something deeper, something unseen but very real.

That moment—though terrifying—was the catalyst for a lifelong connection to my intuitive gifts. It wasn't just about survival; it was about learning to trust that there is something more at play, a force guiding us even in our darkest hours. Over the years, that connection deepened, and I realized that intuition isn't just for rare, dramatic moments. It's a skill, a gift, and most importantly, it's a practice that can be cultivated every day. Whether you're facing a life-altering decision or simply navigating the mundane moments of life, your intuition is always there, offering guidance.

This book is an invitation to reconnect with that part of yourself. You don't need to rely on anyone else to access your inner wisdom. The tools, the knowledge, and the guidance you seek are already within you, waiting to be uncovered. My role is simply to facilitate that journey—to give you the insights, exercises, and encouragement you need to trust yourself more fully.

Through my work as an intuitive healer, psychic medium, and practitioner of past life regression, I've had the honor of helping thousands of people break through their own limiting beliefs and discover the power of their intuition. I've seen firsthand how tapping into your inner knowing can transform your life—bringing you clarity, peace, and a deeper connection to the world around you.

But this journey isn't just about intuition. It's about self-healing. It's about learning to rely on yourself, to trust your own experiences, and to harness the power of your inner voice. We live in a world that often tells us to seek answers from others, but true empowerment comes when you learn to seek answers from within. My mission is to help you do just that.

Over the following chapters, you'll find practical tools to develop your intuition, from creative visualization to recognizing the synchronicities that guide you. You'll also explore the role of transactive memory—how your personal experiences, cultural stories, and even memories from books and films can offer deep intuitive insights.

And for those of you who are ready to take this work to the next level, I invite you to explore some of the offerings I've developed specifically for those on this journey. My **brain entrainment tracks** on Apple and Spotify (Callie Claire) are designed to help you reach deeper states of awareness, aligning your mind with the frequencies of intuition and creativity. I also offer **online courses** on Dream Work & Transactive Memory, on the Sacred Medicine Wheel and **Zoom 12-week certifications** in all aspects of empowerment and intuitive development including evidential mediumship and psychic intuition, where we dive deeper into these practices together, giving you the tools and support you need to develop your gifts. These programs are for anyone who feels called to explore their intuitive abilities further, whether you're just beginning or already on your path.

You are not alone on this journey. Whether you are reading this book for personal growth, healing, or to enhance your intuitive skills, I encourage you to trust that the very fact that you're here means you are ready. You are ready to access the gifts within you, to reconnect with your inner wisdom, and to begin living from a place of trust, love, and self-reliance.

My goal is to remind you that the answers you seek are not out there, but already inside of you. With the tools and guidance offered in this book, and with a little trust in yourself, you can unlock your intuition and use it to create a life that feels aligned, authentic, and truly yours.

YAY!!!! I am so excited you're here!! Let's dive into this journey together.

Callie XO

1

CHAPTER 1:

"Listening to the Whisper: Embracing Your Intuition"

We've all experienced it—that subtle nudge, the soft whisper, or the fleeting feeling that tugs at us before we make a decision. Some call it instinct, others might say it's a gut feeling. For those of us tuned into the spiritual realm, we call it intuition. It's a natural part of who we are, and it's always there, quietly guiding us, if we're willing to listen.

In this chapter, we'll dive into the art of embracing your intuition—not as some mystical force outside of yourself, but as a powerful, everyday tool that can help you navigate life's ups and downs with ease. The beauty of intuition is that it belongs to all of us. Whether you're trying to make a big life decision, picking up on someone's unspoken feelings, or simply trying to find a parking spot, your intuition is there to assist.

Trusting the Quiet Voice

For many, the challenge lies in trusting that quiet voice. In our fast-paced, data-driven world, we've been conditioned to ignore our inner knowing. We second-guess ourselves, doubting our instincts, and relying on logic or external validation. But here's the fun part—when you start to lean into your intuition, it begins to show up in bigger, brighter ways. It's like flexing a muscle—the more you use it, the stronger it becomes.

The best part? Intuition doesn't have to be something grand or dramatic. It might start small, like a gentle pull towards a book you've never heard of or a feeling that today's not the day for that road trip. Trust those nudges. The more you do, the more they'll lead you down paths that feel right and aligned with your true self.

The Joy of Following Your Intuition

One of the most rewarding aspects of following your intuition is the joy it brings. Think about the times you've gone with your gut and everything just clicked. It feels effortless, like you're exactly where you're meant to be, doing exactly what you're supposed to do. That's the magic of intuition—it leads you to your joy, your purpose, and your peace. And as you continue to trust it, you'll find yourself in sync with life in ways that bring more ease and happiness.

You don't need to be psychic to tap into this. Intuition is something we all have—it's the universe's way of helping you out, giving you a head start on figuring things out before they happen. If you've ever felt like you just *knew* something before it happened, that's your intuition at work.

Play with Your Intuition

Here's the fun part: let yourself play! You don't have to treat intuition like a heavy, serious thing. Start light. When you're out shopping, let your gut choose what aisle to walk down first. Test it with small decisions and see what happens. The more you let intuition lead in everyday choices, the easier it becomes to trust in the bigger moments.

By the end of this chapter, you'll have a simple toolkit for recognizing and acting on your intuitive nudges, making life a little more fun, more magical, and infinitely more aligned. So, are you ready to lean into the whisper? Let's go!

"Integrity in Intuition: Why Trust and Authenticity Matter"

In the world of intuitive work, integrity is everything. When you're working with people's energy, emotions, and personal experiences, there is a great responsibility to act with honesty and respect. The foundation of any psychic or spiritual practice should be trust—both in the intuitive process itself and in the person facilitating the journey. Without integrity, the sacred bond between client and facilitator breaks down, and the transformative power of the experience is lost.

For me, this work has always been about helping others heal, grow, and discover their own inner wisdom. I've spent years honing my craft, not just through study but through thousands of hours of one-on-one sessions where I prioritize my clients' well-being above all. As an **intuitive healer**, my role is not to dictate anyone's future or implant ideas, but to hold space for each person to access their own insights, metaphors, and experiences.

Integrity and Duty Matter

With over 10,000 hours of healing work, my experience as a practitioner allows me to guide individuals on their own unique journeys of self-discovery. I don't believe in giving rigid answers or making predictions that foster dependency. Instead, I facilitate a process where the client's own intuition takes the lead. Whether through **past life regression** or intuitive guidance, my focus is always on empowering others to find their truth.

The integrity of my work is rooted in a commitment to facilitating experiences with **compassion**, **non-judgment**, and the highest regard for my clients' personal growth. My intuition is a tool, but it's the client's journey, their insights, and their transformation that matter most. I serve as a steward of the process, guiding individuals to connect with their own higher selves, their spiritual guides, and the unseen forces that are always supporting them.

As you progress through your own blossoming intuitive journey, you will naturally integrate your evolving belief systems to what best suits you. This is a sacred evolutionary process that to me is quite intimately private. Never feel the need to discuss your beliefs, justify them or explain yourself to detractors. Rather groove on the new companions you meet walking parallel pathways.

Integrating Intuition into Everyday Decisions

Practical Intuition: Using Your Inner Wisdom in Daily Life

While intuition can seem mystical or otherworldly, it's actually a highly practical tool that can help guide your decisions in everyday life. Whether you're navigating relationships, making financial choices, or even deciding what to focus on in your career, your intuition is there to support you.

Work Decisions: Let's say you're considering a career shift or a new project at work. Your intuition can offer subtle nudges—like a gut feeling or a clear vision of the potential outcome. By tuning into these insights, you can balance logic and intuition, making decisions that align with your deeper purpose.

Relationships: We all know relationships can be tricky. Whether it's personal or professional, intuition often helps clarify the energy of a situation. When you get a sense that something feels "off" or conversely, when someone feels like the right match for a collaboration or partnership, your intuition is guiding you.

Health and Wellness: From choosing the right nutrition to knowing when to rest, your intuition is a reliable guide in listening to your body's needs. Sometimes the answers aren't in the latest trend or health article—they're in the quiet messages your body sends, guiding you toward balance and well-being.

By incorporating your intuition into these daily decisions, you can move through life with greater ease and clarity, knowing that you are always connected to your inner wisdom.

As you begin to apply your intuition to daily decisions— whether in work, relationships, or health—you'll notice that this inner wisdom often draws from deeper, sometimes unexpected places. Intuition taps into layers of knowledge that go beyond the present moment, connecting you to a broader sense of understanding. This is where the exploration of **past lives as metaphors** comes in. The stories we uncover through past life regression aren't just distant memories; they are rich, symbolic representations of our current experiences. Let's explore how these metaphors can offer profound insight and healing, providing a mirror for the lessons and patterns we're working through in this lifetime.

Why Past Lives are Metaphor and an Introduction to the Akashic Records: Unlocking the Wisdom of the Soul-Self

Sometimes when I'm facilitating a big Past Life Regression parties, my clients will have these vivid pictures and feelings come up. Inevitably they will ask, is it real or just what I wanted to see? My answer is always the same, these visions are akin to dream analysis, and there are lots of juicy tidbits in every sequence we experience. For me personally, these visualizations are cathartic and visceral. For other, for a variety of reasons, they prefer this meditation process to be akin to dream analysis. Whatever perimeters- or lack thereof- you choose to engage upon in this deeply healing process, all roads lead to epiphanies big and small.

For many, the idea of past lives can seem far-fetched. But when you view past life experiences through the lens of metaphor, it becomes a powerful tool for healing and transformation. In my practice, past life regression isn't about proving who you were in a previous life—it's about uncovering the symbolic messages hidden within those experiences. The lives you explore are often metaphors for your current challenges, offering a fresh perspective on how to move forward in this life.

When someone experiences a past life vision as a healer, warrior, or even a victim of betrayal, the emotions and lessons from that life provide clarity for their current journey. It is hugely cathartic. The experiences become metaphors that can help people understand the emotional patterns they carry, the challenges they face, and the strengths they possess. Past life regression, then, is not about literal past lives but about connecting with the deeper, subconscious wisdom of the soul.

Although for some, myself included, the experience of past life regression is visceral and infinitely memorable. It heals all the issues, parental and ancestral, environmental, romantic, even addiction, the more deep rooted the pain, the bigger the epiphany. I use a proprietary mix of intuitive, yogic breathing and neuro-linguistic techniques combined with chakra work and creative visualization in a signature session that my clients say is equivalent to 1, 2, even 3 years (!) of traditional talk therapy.

The strategy of past life regression hypnotherapy is powerful, so I use it with all of my clients and in my online (live) mediumship certification programs. PLR has a prized place in my online courses and brain entrainment albums because *by far*, it is the best strategy for healing deep-rooted pain than I have personally ever experienced or utilized on behalf of others.

So, while it may seem totally woo-woo, we are in fact being hypnotized all the time- TV, doom scrolling on Instagram, that smoochy romance movie all grab our subconscious attention via a mild and highly suggestible hypnosis state. This process relies on tapping into your innate wisdom- super empowering.

By the way, if someone is charging you top dollar to tell you who you were in a past life, that's the opposite of what past life regression hypnotherapy was designed to do- empower you!

The Akashic Records: A Metaphysical Library

As you wander your own unique path, and as you work with me, the topic of the **Akashic records** are sure to come up. So, what are they? As in everything, this soul crucible is many things to many people.

A mystical, dream life place often described as a metaphysical library—a cosmic archive of every thought, action, and experience of every soul throughout time. For those who believe in reincarnation or the continuity of the soul, the Akashic records represent an infinite source of knowledge. Tapping into these records allows people to access the soul's collective wisdom, uncover hidden patterns, and gain insight into their soul's purpose.

My own personal experiences with this occurred in the dream realm as a child and teen, then I tapped into those same experiences during brain entrainment meditations later on. This does bring us full circle to the mysterious realm of dreams, and the repetitive patterns our dream history continue to show us in good times and bad.

The Akashic Records and dream time are both realms where the soul can access profound wisdom and insight. The Akashic Records, often described as a cosmic library of every thought, action, and experience across all lifetimes, mirrors the expansiveness of dream time, where the boundaries of the conscious mind dissolve. In both, we find ourselves tapping into a deeper knowing, where past, present, and future merge into a singular truth. Just as our dreams provide guidance and reflection from our subconscious, the Akashic Records offer a roadmap of the soul's journey. Both invite us to explore beyond the veil of ordinary awareness and to receive the whispers of our higher selves, the collective consciousness, and the universe. In this way, dream time can be seen as a key to unlocking the wisdom of the Akashic Records, allowing us to integrate these spiritual insights into our waking life.

The Akashic records are not restricted by time. They offer a view of the soul's entire journey, across lifetimes and dimensions. In my work, I see these records as a way of understanding the broader lessons we are here to learn. Many of us naturally experience this knowledge in daily life, whether you are a devotee of 'being in the moment', if in a moment of reflection at church or on a nature walk you are struck by the synchronicity and metaphor of life, you understand the power of exquisite listening.

For others seeking to connect with their own inner wisdom, the path to holistic healing might hold more out-of-the-box possibilities. Whether through past life regression, intuitive downloads, or simply meditation, accessing this higher knowledge helps people recognize the deeper purpose behind their current challenges. We will circle back to this concept when we discuss the fascinating psychic-psychological concept of Transactive Memory later on in this book.

* * * * *

Chapter 1 Summary: "Listening to the Whisper: Embracing Your Intuition," introduces intuition as a natural, everyday tool available to everyone. It encourages readers to trust their inner guidance, that subtle nudge often referred to as a gut feeling or instinct. By listening to these quiet signals, we can navigate life's decisions more effortlessly and align with our true selves. The more we trust and use our intuition, the stronger and clearer it becomes, helping us not only with small daily choices but also with major life decisions.

The chapter also emphasizes the importance of integrity in intuitive work, stressing that the role of intuition is to empower, not dictate. By cultivating a deep connection with our inner knowing, we can move through life with greater ease, joy, and purpose, while staying true to our authentic selves.

CHAPTER 2:

"Everyday Magic: Bringing Intuition into Your Daily Life"

Now that we've explored the whispers of intuition, it's time to see how it can show up in your day-to-day routine. Contrary to popular belief, intuition doesn't have to feel mystical or reserved for life-changing decisions. It's something you can tap into every day—whether you're choosing what to make for dinner, which direction to take on your walk, or how to approach that big project at work.

Think of intuition as your personal assistant, always in the background, waiting to be called upon. It's like having an inner GPS that's always recalculating your route to match the best outcome for you. And the best part? There's no limit to how often you can use it.

Start Your Day with Intuition

Let's begin with the first moments of your day. How do you usually wake up? Maybe you jump straight into a flurry of thoughts about your to-do list. But what if, instead, you took a moment to check in with your intuition?

Before your feet hit the floor, pause and take a breath. Ask yourself, "How do I want to feel today? What feels most aligned for me right now?" Allow your intuition to guide your morning choices. Maybe it's suggesting a walk outside instead of your usual coffee, or perhaps today's the day you call that friend who's been on your mind. When you start your day connected to your inner wisdom, everything flows more smoothly.

Decisions Big and Small

We make countless decisions every day. Some seem trivial, while others weigh on us a little more heavily. Here's where intuition can make all the difference. For smaller decisions, like what to eat or which route to take to work, let your intuition lead the way. If you feel a sudden urge to take a different path home, go with it—you never know what kind of serendipity might be waiting around the corner.

For bigger decisions, like choosing a new job or moving to a new city, it's normal to feel overwhelmed by all the options. This is where intuition steps in as a guiding light. Instead of listing out pros and cons, take a moment to get quiet and feel into each option. Does one feel lighter? More exciting? Trust those feelings. Your intuition knows the path that will bring you the most fulfillment, even if it's not immediately obvious to your logical mind.

Intuition in Relationships

Relationships, both personal and professional, can be one of the trickiest areas to navigate. Intuition plays a key role in understanding others and recognizing what's unsaid. Think of all the times you've felt that something was "off" in a conversation, even though the other person was saying all the right things. That's your intuition giving you insight into their true feelings.

When you listen to your intuition in relationships, you become a better communicator. You can sense when to push forward and when to pull back. You're also better at reading your own needs—knowing when you need space or when it's time to reach out for support.

Intuition helps you navigate these delicate interactions with grace, preventing misunderstandings before they escalate and helping you feel more confident in your choices.

Tuning In Through Creativity

Creative activities—whether painting, writing, cooking, or gardening—are wonderful ways to engage your intuition. When you let go of rigid expectations and allow yourself to flow, you tap into a deeper source of inspiration. Creativity quiets the noise in your mind and opens you up to intuitive insight.

As an artist and designer, I've found that some of my best work comes when I allow my intuition to guide the process. Instead of forcing a specific outcome, I let the work unfold naturally, and the results are often more magical than I could have planned. Try it out next time you're working on a project—let your intuition take the lead and watch what unfolds.

Living Intuitively: A Daily Practice

Intuition is like a muscle; the more you use it, the stronger it becomes. It's about incorporating it into your everyday life, letting it flow into everything you do. Instead of overthinking every step, trust that gentle pull inside you. Over time, you'll find that life flows more easily, and the decisions that once seemed hard become second nature.

Calling on Angel Guides, Saints, and Historical Figures

Many people feel a strong affinity for angelic guides, saints, or historical figures whose life stories resonate deeply with sacred truths in their hearts. These guides offer powerful support, and it can be incredibly beneficial to call on them in times of strain, trouble, or doubt. Whether it's an angel whose presence feels comforting, a saint known for their wisdom and grace, or a historical figure who embodies resilience and strength, these spiritual allies provide profound guidance and protection.

I had my own unforgettable experience with a spiritual guide during a time when my intuitive gifts were developing at an exponential pace. While using brain entrainment, I had a vivid vision of climbing stairs and encountering a magnificent Native American in full regalia. The vision was so powerful that it left me in awe. After a deep, restorative sleep, I awoke refreshed and began my usual morning routine. As I looked out of my kitchen window at the long, narrow backyard of my 175-year-old brick federal townhouse, to my utter shock, I saw the holographic figure of the Native American man from my vision. With a cheeky grin, he beat his chest like Tarzan, waved at me, and walked through the fence as if he belonged there.

Was it real? I was just sipping my Irish breakfast tea and smiling at the birds, but the experience left an undeniable mark on me. I had never seen anything like it before or since, but I'm so grateful I did that day. It gave me a sense of fulfillment, security, and a dash of mystery—reminding me that these spiritual connections, whether angelic or ancestral, are always there to offer guidance when we are open to receiving it.

***

The connection between angelic guidance, saintly wisdom, and intuition is deeply intertwined with **the practice of non-judgment.** When we call upon angels, saints, or historical figures for guidance, their presence often brings a sense of unconditional love and acceptance. This divine energy teaches us to approach ourselves and others with greater compassion. By fostering non-judgment, we create space for our intuition to flourish, allowing us to receive messages from these higher sources without the interference of personal bias or limiting beliefs. As we open ourselves to this form of guidance, we also cultivate a more open, compassionate heart, one that embraces others as they are and receives divine wisdom with clarity and grace. And of course, judgment acts as a mirror, a reflection of how ee view others. It is worthy of reverent consideration on your path.

A Life of Clarity and Resilience is Key

So why do I focus on clarity and resilience?

In my journey, I've always chosen to live with clarity, avoiding drugs and alcohol, and only began taking medication during perimenopause when it became necessary. At the beginning, it was because I wanted to main control- which is fair.

Now, after decades of following what the Buddhists might call the path of moderation, this choice has been a cornerstone in my ability to manifest success in both my life and career. Through this clear-headed approach, I've been able to navigate significant challenges, including the deeply personal experience of a dozen miscarriages. Despite those losses, I was blessed to manifest my children, a testament to the power of perseverance, faith, and resilience.

It's important to recognize how living a life of clarity allows us to tune into our inner guidance, staying aligned with our purpose. The ability to achieve great things, both personally and professionally, often requires this level of dedication and self-awareness. By staying grounded and clear, I've been able to manifest not only my family but also a fulfilling career that aligns with my gifts and passions. This path, though difficult at times, has taught me the value of resilience, determination, and the strength that comes from living a life rooted in clarity.

At the end of the day, I get paid to focus my attention on focusing your attention. So, to keep my body (that thing that houses my soul) fit, and I also keep my house-body, that thing that houses my soul-in-body fit, too!

I do all the boring basics, getting eight hours of sleep a night, swimming, walking and yoga, cooking delish healthy meals, cleaning and decluttering and adding cheer to create a solid foundation to let my wildflowers grow!

Strengthening your physical foundation is a great place to start when your world is topsy-turvy.

$$* * * * *$$

Chapter 2 Summary: "Everyday Magic: Bringing Intuition into Your Daily Life," emphasizes that intuition isn't reserved for extraordinary moments—it's a tool that can guide us through everyday decisions, big or small. From choosing how to start your morning to deciding on a major life change, intuition acts as an internal GPS, constantly recalibrating to help you find the best path forward. By integrating intuitive guidance into daily routines, you can create a smoother, more aligned life where decisions flow naturally.

The chapter also explores how intuition can enhance relationships, creativity, and personal well-being. Whether navigating delicate conversations or tapping into creative endeavors, trusting your intuitive instincts opens up new possibilities and deeper understanding. By treating intuition as a playful, everyday practice, rather than a rare gift, you strengthen it over time, allowing it to bring more clarity and ease into all areas of your life.

CHAPTER 3:

"Decoding the Signs: How Intuition Speaks to You"

By now, you've started to feel the gentle nudges of your intuition and maybe even taken a few playful leaps into trusting it. But how does intuition communicate with us? Does it speak in words, feelings, or something else entirely? In this chapter, we'll explore the different ways intuition shows up in your life and how to decode the signs that are constantly guiding you.

Intuition Speaks in Many Languages

The fascinating thing about intuition is that it doesn't have one universal voice. It's as unique as you are, and it will find ways to speak to you that resonate with your personality and life experiences. Some people get a gut feeling, while others might hear a soft inner voice. For some, it's vivid imagery that appears in their mind's eye, and for others, it's simply a sense of knowing.

One thing's for sure—intuition is always communicating. Sometimes, it's subtle: a quick flash of insight, an unexpected song lyric that seems to answer a question, or a feeling of ease when making a decision. Other times, it's a loud, clear signal that practically shouts, "Go this way!"

So how do you know which signs are intuitive and which are just random? It all comes down to feeling.

Trust Your Feelings, Not Just Your Thoughts

Feelings are one of the most powerful ways intuition speaks. Remember that the word emotion means E + Motion= Energy in Motion.

Have you ever had that feeling where something just didn't sit right, even though everything seemed fine on the surface? Or maybe you felt an inexplicable sense of calm in a situation where others might have panicked. These feelings are your intuition's way of guiding you.

When you're tuning in to your intuitive feelings, start by paying attention to your body. Do you feel tension in your chest when you think about a particular decision? Or maybe a sense of lightness in your stomach when you consider a new opportunity. Intuition often shows up as sensations in the body—these are your inner signals telling you what feels aligned and what doesn't.

It's important to note that intuitive feelings are different from fear or anxiety. Intuition has a way of being clear and calm, even in the midst of uncertainty. Fear, on the other hand, tends to create confusion or a sense of urgency. The more you practice feeling into your decisions, the easier it becomes to distinguish between the two.

The Language of Synchronicity

Synchronicity is another way intuition gets your attention. These are the meaningful coincidences that feel like the universe is winking at you, letting you know you're on the right track. Have you ever thought about someone and then they suddenly call you out of the blue? Or maybe you've been thinking about changing careers, and then you keep seeing ads, articles, or opportunities related to that new path.

These synchronicities are not just random events; they are signals from the universe, guiding you toward what's in alignment with your higher self. When you start noticing patterns like these, take them as confirmation that your intuition is speaking to you and nudging you in the right direction.

Listening to Your Inner Voice

For some, intuition shows up as a quiet inner voice. It's not the kind of voice you hear with your ears but one that seems to come from deep within. This voice is often calm, wise, and reassuring. It doesn't ramble or repeat itself; it speaks clearly and directly.

One of the best ways to strengthen your connection to this inner voice is through practices like meditation or journaling. When you quiet your mind and create space for stillness, you're more likely to hear the subtle guidance that's always there, waiting to be acknowledged.

Next time you have a big decision to make, take a few moments to sit in silence. Ask yourself, "What feels right?" and listen for the answer that comes. It might not be loud or dramatic, but if you listen closely, you'll hear it.

Signs from the World Around You

Intuition doesn't always come from within; sometimes, it shows up in the world around you. Nature, for example, is full of intuitive signs. Have you ever noticed how animals seem to sense things long before humans do? Birds taking flight before a storm or a dog barking at someone with bad energy—these are natural, intuitive reactions.

You, too, can learn to pick up on these external cues. Maybe you see a specific animal repeatedly or a certain number keeps appearing. The universe loves to communicate through symbols, and your job is to start noticing them. Pay attention to recurring signs—whether it's through nature, numbers, or even messages in books or conversations. If something feels significant, it probably is.

Making Space for Signs and Signals

One of the best ways to invite more intuitive signs into your life is by creating space for them. In our busy, modern lives, it's easy to overlook these subtle cues. But when you intentionally slow down and create moments of stillness, you allow the universe to communicate more clearly.

Here's a simple exercise: start each day by asking for guidance. It doesn't have to be formal or complicated. You can simply say, "I'm open to signs today—please guide me in the right direction." Then, go about your day with an open mind, noticing any feelings, signs, or synchronicities that show up. Keep a journal to track these moments, and over time, you'll start to see just how often your intuition is at work.

* * * * *

Chapter 3 Summary: Your intuition speaks in many languages—through feelings, synchronicities, inner voices, and the world around you. By learning to recognize these signs and signals, you strengthen your ability to live an intuitive, aligned life. Whether through a soft whisper or a clear, undeniable sign, your intuition is always guiding you. The key is to stay open and pay attention.

~ 28 ~

CHAPTER 4:

"Unlocking Intuition: Practical Tools to Strengthen Your Inner Knowing"

At this point, you've started to feel the subtle nudges of your intuition, and you're beginning to notice how it shows up in your daily life. Now, it's time to take things up a notch. In this chapter, we'll explore some powerful yet simple tools that will help you consciously strengthen your intuitive abilities. These are practices you can incorporate into your routine, allowing your intuition to become a trusted companion in every decision you make.

1. Meditation: The Gateway to Intuition

Meditation is one of the most effective ways to clear your mental clutter and make room for intuitive insights. When

~ 29 ~

your mind is constantly racing with thoughts, worries, and to-do lists, it can be hard to hear that quiet inner voice. Meditation helps you create space for stillness, which is where intuition thrives.

Don't worry—you don't need to sit in silence for hours to get results. Even five minutes a day can make a world of difference. Here's a simple meditation to try:

- Find a quiet space where you won't be disturbed.
- Close your eyes and take a few deep breaths.
- Focus on your breath, feeling it move in and out of your body.
- If your mind starts to wander, gently bring it back to your breath.
- After a few minutes, ask yourself a question: "What do I need to know right now?"
- Sit quietly and see what thoughts or feelings come up. Don't force anything—just stay open.

With regular practice, you'll find that your mind becomes quieter, and your intuition begins to speak more clearly.

2. Journaling: Writing Your Way to Clarity

If meditation is the gateway, journaling is the map. When you put pen to paper, you engage both your logical mind and your intuitive self, creating a bridge between the two. Journaling allows you to process your thoughts and emotions, making space for deeper insights to surface.

Try this intuitive journaling exercise:

- Set aside 10-15 minutes in the morning or before bed.

- Write down any questions or challenges you're currently facing.

- Now, write from the perspective of your intuition. What does your inner wisdom have to say? It might feel a little strange at first, but go with it. Let the words flow without judgment.

- You might be surprised at the insights that come through—answers you hadn't considered, solutions that feel lighter and more aligned.

Over time, this practice will help you access your intuition more easily, even in the middle of busy days.

3. Trusting Your First Impressions

One of the simplest yet most effective ways to strengthen your intuition is by learning to trust your first impressions. Often, our initial reaction to a situation or person is the most intuitive one, but we quickly second-guess ourselves, letting doubt or logic take over.

Here's an exercise to practice:

- The next time you meet someone new or face a decision, pause and take a mental note of your very first impression. What's your gut reaction?

- Now, before you analyze or question it, trust that feeling. Give yourself permission to act on it, even if it doesn't make sense at first.

You'll start to notice that your first impressions are often spot-on, and by trusting them, you strengthen your intuitive muscle.

4. Grounding Yourself: Staying Connected to the Earth

Intuition flows best when you're grounded—physically and energetically. Grounding is the practice of connecting to the earth, bringing your energy back into balance, and creating a sense of stability.

There are many simple ways to ground yourself:

- Take a walk in nature, paying attention to the sights, sounds, and smells around you.
- Sit on the ground, grass, or sand, and feel the earth beneath you.
- Practice deep breathing, imagining your energy roots extending deep into the ground.

By grounding yourself regularly, you create a stable foundation for intuitive insights to flow. You'll feel more centered, balanced, and open to receiving guidance.

5. Play with Your Intuition: Fun Exercises to Sharpen Your Senses

Who says strengthening your intuition can't be fun? Incorporating play into your intuitive practice not only makes it more enjoyable but also helps you get out of your own way.

Try these playful exercises to tap into your intuitive side:

- **Card Games:** Shuffle a deck of playing cards and guess the suit or color of the next card before flipping it over. This helps you get used to trusting your first instinct.

- **Guessing Game:** Next time your phone rings, take a moment before looking at the screen and see if you can intuitively sense who's calling. With practice, you'll start to get it right more often than not!

- **Choose Your Path:** The next time you're out for a walk, let your intuition guide you. Don't overthink it—just go where you feel drawn. You might discover something unexpected, whether it's a beautiful view, an interesting conversation, or a new idea.

The more you play with your intuition, the more natural it will feel to rely on it in everyday situations.

6. Listening to Your Body: Physical Intuition

Your body is a powerful tool for intuition. Often, it picks up on energy and signals long before your mind does. Learning to listen to your body's cues is an essential part of developing your intuitive abilities.

Here's how to start:

- Notice how your body feels when you think about a specific situation or decision. Do you feel tense or relaxed? Energized or drained?

- Pay attention to any physical sensations you experience throughout the day—tingling, tightness, warmth, or heaviness. These are all signs that your body is picking up on something energetically.

- Trust these physical cues and use them to guide your actions. Your body knows what's best for you, and it's always communicating that wisdom through subtle signals.

The Power of Play: How Joy Enhances Your Intuition

While spirituality and intuition are deeply intertwined and mystically meaningful, they don't have to be solemn. In fact, **joy and play** are powerful catalysts for intuitive growth. When you laugh, play, and tap into your inner child, you open yourself up to new possibilities and spontaneous insights. Playfulness quiets the critical mind, allowing your intuitive mind to shine.

Creative Play: Whether it's painting, dancing, or trying something new like improv, creativity sparks intuitive growth. It's no coincidence that many intuitive people and spiritual teachers also engage in creative pursuits. When you're in a state of joy, you're more likely to receive clear intuitive downloads.

Lighthearted Curiosity: Approach your spiritual journey with curiosity and a sense of fun. Rather than feeling like you need to "master" intuition, enjoy the process of discovery. The lighter and more open you are, the more natural the insights will flow. After all, intuition thrives in an atmosphere of joy and wonder.

By embracing joy and play as part of your intuitive practice, you unlock a deeper sense of flow, where intuition becomes part of your everyday rhythm—without the pressure to get it "right."

* * * * *

Chapter 4 Summary: Strengthening your intuition doesn't have to be complicated. With simple practices like meditation, journaling, and playing intuitive games, you can tune in to your inner guidance in a way that feels natural and fun. By grounding yourself and listening to your body, you create a stable foundation for your intuitive abilities to flourish. The more you trust and use these tools, the more intuition will become a reliable part of your everyday life.

CHAPTER 5:

"Signs from the Universe: Recognizing the Messages All Around You"

Life has a way of speaking to us through signs and symbols— tiny breadcrumbs left by the universe to guide us toward our highest path. These signs can show up in everyday moments, but the key is knowing how to recognize them and trust that they are meant for you. In this chapter, we'll explore how to identify the signs from the universe and use them to inform your decisions, spark your creativity, and deepen your intuitive practice.

The Universe is Always Speaking—Are You Listening?

Have you ever noticed how certain numbers, songs, or animals seem to appear just when you need them? Maybe you've been thinking about making a big life change, and suddenly you see the same number pattern—like 11:11—repeated everywhere. Or you're feeling stuck, and a song comes on the radio that speaks directly to your situation.

These are not random coincidences; they are the universe's way of communicating with you. The signs are always there, but to fully benefit from them, you need to be open and willing to listen. Signs often come when we're asking for guidance but unsure of which direction to take. When you start paying attention to these moments, you'll realize the universe is always offering help—you just need to tune in.

How to Recognize Signs from the Universe

The first step in recognizing signs is to cultivate a sense of awareness. Often, we're so caught up in our thoughts that we miss the subtle nudges the universe is sending us. Here are some common ways the universe speaks:

- **Number Patterns:** Repeating numbers like 11:11, 222, or 333 often indicate that you're aligned with your higher path. These patterns can signal new beginnings, affirmations of support, or a reminder that you're not alone.

- **Songs or Lyrics:** Music has a way of carrying messages, especially when you're emotionally tuned in. Pay attention to song lyrics that seem to appear at just the right moment—whether it's a lyric about love, resilience, or taking a leap of faith, it's often a direct message for you.

- **Animals and Nature:** Animals and nature can serve as powerful symbols. If you keep encountering the same animal (whether in real life or through images), look up its spiritual meaning. Nature often mirrors our own experiences and offers clues about where we are in our journey.

- **Random Conversations or Words:** Sometimes, you might overhear a conversation or see a phrase in a book or on a billboard that feels oddly relevant. These moments are often the universe's way of getting your attention and confirming your thoughts or ideas.

When a Sign Feels Personal

Some signs just hit differently—they feel more intimate, more personal. You might be thinking about a loved one who's passed, and suddenly a butterfly lands nearby, or you see a reminder of something that was meaningful between you. These personal signs carry a strong emotional resonance, and they're often a message of love or encouragement from the other side.

Don't dismiss these experiences as mere coincidences. Trust your intuition when a sign feels personal. It's your inner knowing recognizing that the universe is speaking directly to you.

How to Ask for a Sign

If you're seeking guidance on a specific issue and want a clear sign, you can always ask the universe for one. The key is to be open, patient, and specific without attaching to the outcome. Here's how to ask:

1. Get quiet and focus on the question or area of your life where you need guidance.
2. Ask the universe to send you a clear, undeniable sign that aligns with your highest good.
3. Let go of the need for immediate answers. The sign may come in an unexpected way—so keep your awareness open in the days that follow.

For example, if you're trying to make a career decision, you might ask for a sign that confirms whether you should stay or move on. The sign could show up as a random conversation, a job offer, or even a specific image that brings clarity.

Ask with love, patience, and specificity.

Journaling to Decode Signs

Once you start noticing signs, it's helpful to keep track of them. Journaling is a great way to reflect on the signs you receive and what they mean to you. Here's a simple format to follow:

- **Date & Time:** When did you receive the sign?
- **The Sign:** Describe the sign in detail—whether it was a number, song, or something else.
- **Your Feelings:** How did the sign make you feel? Did it spark joy, calm, or curiosity?

- **Possible Meaning:** Reflect on what the sign could be telling you. Does it confirm something you've been thinking about, or does it offer a new perspective?

By writing down your experiences, you begin to see patterns emerge, helping you connect the dots between the signs and the decisions you're facing.

The Balance Between Signs and Free Will

While signs are helpful guides, it's important to remember that they are just that—guides. You always have free will, and the ultimate power to shape your life lies within you. Signs can provide clarity and confirmation, but they aren't meant to take away your ability to choose. Trust your intuition and combine it with the signs you receive to make decisions that feel right for you.

Signs as a Reflection of Your Energy

It's also worth noting that the signs you see often reflect your current state of energy. When you're feeling open, aligned, and in a positive mindset, you'll notice more uplifting and encouraging signs. On the other hand, if you're feeling stressed or disconnected, the signs might feel more like warnings or red flags.

This is why grounding and clearing your energy regularly is so important. The more you're in tune with your inner self, the clearer and more aligned the signs from the universe become.

Choosing a Trusted Spirit Guide for Your Journey

When embarking on your dream or meditation journey, it's important to feel safe and protected as you explore the deeper realms of consciousness. One powerful way to do this is by choosing a trusted spirit guide—someone who can serve as your steward, watching over you as you navigate these inner landscapes. This guide could be a beloved grandparent, a departed friend, or another relative who has passed on but remains close to your heart.

To connect with your guide, start by taking a few moments in stillness, either before bed or during meditation. As you focus on your breath, allow yourself to relax deeply. Then, call upon the presence of your chosen guide, imagining their warmth and love surrounding you. Feel their protective energy enveloping you, offering a sense of safety and wisdom as you journey inward. Trust that this guide is there to watch over you, ensuring that the insights and experiences you encounter align with your highest good.

By inviting this spirit guide into your dreams and meditations, you create a sacred partnership that offers protection, guidance, and support. With their presence, you can journey deeper, knowing that you are not alone but are accompanied by a loving soul who has your best interests at heart.

I recommend a loved one who has departed or an angel you feel connected to rather than a pet, but do what feels best in your heart!

* * * * *

Chapter 5 Summary: The universe is constantly communicating with you through signs and symbols. By developing a sense of awareness and being open to these messages, you can strengthen your intuitive practice and receive valuable guidance in your life. Whether through numbers, nature, music, angelic guides or personal signs, the universe always has your back. Remember, signs are here to guide, not dictate—your free will is the ultimate force behind the choices you make.

CHAPTER 6:

"The Intuitive Body: Listening to Your Physical Wisdom"

Your body is an incredible intuitive tool, constantly sending you signals that can guide you through life's challenges and opportunities. From the subtle sensation of tension in your shoulders when something feels off, to the lightness in your heart when you're aligned with a decision, your body is speaking to you all the time. In this chapter, we'll dive deep into how your physical body plays a crucial role in your intuitive journey, and how to listen to its wisdom.

Your Body Knows Before You Do

Have you ever noticed how your body reacts before your mind catches up? Maybe your heart starts to race before you even realize you're feeling nervous, or you get a sudden chill when you walk into a room with heavy energy. These are signs that your body is picking up on information that your conscious mind hasn't yet processed.

Your body is like an antenna for energy, constantly scanning your environment and your emotions. It reacts to people, places, and situations long before your brain has a chance to analyze them. Learning to listen to these physical cues is one of the most reliable ways to strengthen your intuition.

How to Tune Into Your Body's Intuition

One of the most powerful ways to sharpen your intuitive connection is by becoming more aware of how your body feels in different situations. Here's a simple practice to help you tune in:

1. **Pause and Breathe:** Whenever you're faced with a decision or feel unsure about something, pause and take a deep breath. Close your eyes if it helps you focus.
2. **Scan Your Body:** Start at your head and slowly scan down to your feet. Notice any areas of tension, warmth, coolness, or tingling. These sensations are your body's way of communicating with you.

3. **Ask Your Body for Guidance:** Once you've tuned in, ask your body how it feels about the situation. If you're deciding between two options, notice which one feels lighter or more relaxed in your body. Which one makes you feel tense or uneasy?

4. **Trust the Physical Reaction:** Even if your logical mind is telling you something different, trust how your body feels. Physical intuition is often more accurate than overthinking, especially when you're dealing with something emotional or uncertain.

The Gut-Brain Connection: Trusting Your Gut Feelings

You've likely heard the phrase "trust your gut," but there's real science behind it. The gut-brain connection is a well-documented phenomenon, where your digestive system acts as a second brain, constantly communicating with your central nervous system. That "gut feeling" you get when something feels right—or wrong—isn't just a metaphor; it's a physiological response.

When your gut feels tight, queasy, or uncomfortable, it's your body's way of telling you that something is off. Conversely, when you feel relaxed or at ease in your stomach, it's often a sign that you're in alignment with your intuition. The key is to learn to recognize and trust these feelings, even when your mind wants to override them.

Physical Signs of Alignment

When you're in tune with your intuition, your body will often give you physical signs of alignment. These can show up as feelings of lightness, warmth, or even a tingly sensation when you're making a decision that's right for you. Some people describe it as a sense of "flow," where everything just feels easy and natural.

Here are a few common physical signs that you're aligned with your intuition:

- **A sense of calm or peace** when thinking about a decision or path forward.
- **A feeling of lightness or expansion** in your chest or heart area.
- **A warm, tingly sensation** in your hands or feet.
- **Deep, steady breathing**, indicating that your body feels safe and grounded.

These sensations are your body's way of saying, "Yes, this is right." When you notice them, trust that you're moving in the right direction.

When Your Body Says No: Red Flags and Warnings

Just as your body will give you positive signals when something is right, it will also send you warning signs when something is off. These red flags might show up as physical discomfort, such as:

- **Tightness in the chest or stomach** when thinking about a person, place, or decision.

- **A sudden headache or dizziness** when you're in a stressful environment.

- **Shallow breathing** or a feeling of constriction in your throat.

- **Tension in your shoulders or neck**, often signaling that you're carrying too much stress or responsibility.

When you notice these physical signs, don't ignore them. They are your body's way of alerting you to something that isn't aligned with your highest good. Take a step back, breathe, and reassess the situation before moving forward.

Energy and Movement: Using Your Body to Shift Intuition

Sometimes, we need to actively move our bodies to get clarity. When you feel stuck or unable to access your intuition, physical movement can help you reconnect. Whether it's taking a walk, practicing yoga, or dancing around the living room, moving your body shifts stagnant energy and opens up your intuitive channels.

Here's a fun exercise to try:

1. **Move with Intention:** Set an intention to receive clarity or guidance before you start moving. It could be something like, "I'm open to receiving insight on my next step."

2. **Move Freely:** Let your body move in whatever way feels natural. This isn't about structured exercise—it's about allowing your body to guide the movement. You might sway, stretch, or jump; just let it flow.

3. **Pay Attention to Insights:** As you move, pay attention to any thoughts, feelings, or physical sensations that arise. Often, the act of moving helps you release mental blocks and gain new perspectives.

4. **Journal Your Insights:** After moving, take a few minutes to write down any insights or feelings that came up. You'll likely find that you're able to access your intuition more easily after shifting your physical energy.

The Mind-Body-Intuition Connection

Your body is deeply connected to your mind and spirit. When you take care of your physical self, you're also nourishing your intuitive self. Practices like grounding, breathwork, and mindful movement all contribute to a healthy intuitive flow.

By honoring your body's signals and working with its wisdom, you create a deeper connection to your inner knowing. The more you trust and listen to your body, the more confident you'll become in making intuitive choices that lead you to your best life.

* * * * *

Chapter 6 Summary: Your body is a powerful tool for intuition, constantly sending you signals that can guide you in the right direction. By tuning into your physical sensations, you can access a deeper level of wisdom that complements your logical mind. From trusting your gut feelings to recognizing signs of alignment or red flags, your body is always communicating with you. By integrating practices like movement, grounding, and breathwork, you can strengthen your connection to your physical intuition and make choices that feel right in both mind and body.

CHAPTER 7:

"Synchronicity:
The Universe's Perfect Timing"

Some of the most magical moments in life happen when you least expect them—those uncanny coincidences where everything seems to fall into place in the most mysterious way. That's synchronicity: the universe's way of confirming that you're aligned with your path and offering you guidance along the way. In this chapter, we'll explore how to recognize synchronicities, what they mean, and how they can lead you deeper into your intuitive practice.

What is Synchronicity?

Synchronicity is often described as a meaningful coincidence— events that are connected not by direct cause and effect, but by deeper, symbolic meaning. When synchronicities happen, it feels as though the universe is weaving together unrelated threads of life in perfect harmony. It's like a nudge from the cosmos, saying, *"Yes, you're on the right track. Keep going!"*

These moments of synchronicity can show up in many forms. You might meet someone at the exact moment you need their advice, or you may repeatedly encounter the same symbol or number, signaling a message you need to pay attention to. When synchronicity occurs, it's a powerful reminder that life is always working with you, guiding you toward your highest good.

Recognizing Synchronicity in Your Life

Synchronicity often shows up when you're deeply connected to your intuition and open to receiving guidance from the universe. The more you trust and follow your intuitive nudges, the more synchronicities will appear, like road signs directing you on your journey.

Here's how to recognize synchronicities in your life:

- **Repeating Symbols or Numbers:** If you keep seeing the same symbol, number, or animal in different contexts, it's a sign the universe is trying to communicate something important. For example, seeing 11:11 repeatedly or encountering butterflies everywhere may signal a transformation in your life.

- **Serendipitous Encounters:** Have you ever met someone out of the blue who had the exact knowledge or connection you needed at that moment? These "chance" encounters are often synchronicities in disguise, meant to guide you toward your next step.

- **Perfect Timing:** Sometimes, synchronicity shows up as perfect timing—just when you need something, the solution appears. Whether it's an opportunity, a book, or a person, these moments of perfect timing are the universe's way of showing you that you're in sync with your life's flow.

Embracing Synchronicity: How to Invite More into Your Life

Synchronicity happens most when you're in a state of flow—when you're living in alignment with your purpose and trusting your intuition. To invite more synchronicities into your life, you need to create space for them. Here are a few ways to embrace and cultivate synchronicity:

- **Stay Open:** Keep an open mind and heart. Often, we dismiss synchronicities because they don't fit into our logical understanding of the world. But the more open you are to the idea that the universe communicates through signs and coincidences, the more you'll notice them.

- **Ask for Guidance:** Don't be afraid to ask the universe for signs. When you're facing a big decision or need clarity on your next step, put your intention out there and ask for a synchronistic confirmation. Then, pay attention to what shows up in the days that follow.

- **Be Present:** Synchronicity often occurs when you're fully present in the moment, not distracted by worries or overthinking. By practicing mindfulness and staying grounded in the here and now, you'll be more attuned to the synchronicities unfolding around you.

As you begin to notice and trust the synchronicities that unfold in your life, you may start to wonder: *Is everything meant to be?* Or *is there room for spontaneity and chance in this grand design?* This is where the delicate dance between **fate** and **chance** comes into play. While synchronicities feel like the universe guiding you with purpose, fate and chance often work together behind the scenes, shaping the direction of your life in ways both destined and delightfully unexpected. Let's explore how these two forces intertwine and how your intuition helps you navigate their subtle rhythms.

Fate and Chance: How They Dance in the Intuitive World

One of the great mysteries we all face is the question of fate versus chance. Are our lives already written, or are we co-writing them as we go along? As you explore your intuitive gifts, this question may arise time and again: *Was this meant to be, or did it just happen by chance?*

Let's dive into the idea that **fate and chance** aren't opposing forces—they're dance partners, working together to shape the story of our lives. Fate is often seen as the big picture—the grand plan the universe or your soul mapped out before you even arrived here. But within that plan, there's plenty of room for **chance**—those unexpected twists, turns, and "happy accidents" that shape your daily life.

Think of **synchronicity** as the cosmic clue that fate and chance are playing together. When events seem too perfectly aligned to be random, that's the universe giving you a wink. It's fate nudging you forward while chance adds its sparkle. Intuition helps you recognize the moments when fate is guiding you and when chance is delivering an opportunity— whether it's meeting the right person at the right time or stumbling across a book that changes your perspective.

In the end, fate may lay the groundwork, but chance invites you to **participate** in the creation of your life. Your intuition acts as the compass, guiding you through both fated events and chance encounters with equal grace.

Vision Quest: A Deeper Connection to Your Intuition

A vision quest is a powerful way to deepen your connection with your intuition and invite even more synchronicity into your life. Traditionally, a vision quest is a rite of passage, where you spend time in solitude, fasting, and communing with nature to receive guidance and insight from the spirit world. While you don't need to go to the wilderness to experience a vision quest, you can create your own version to tap into your intuitive guidance.

Here's how to embark on a simple vision quest:

1. **Set Your Intention:** Before you begin, take time to clarify what you want to gain from the experience. Are you seeking clarity on a specific decision, or are you looking for a deeper connection to your intuition?

2. **Create a Sacred Space:** Find a quiet, peaceful place where you won't be disturbed. This could be a spot in nature, your home, or even a cozy corner in your garden. Set up your space with items that inspire you, such as candles, crystals, or journal.

3. **Listen to Your Inner Guidance:** Spend time in stillness and solitude. You might want to meditate, journal, or simply sit in silence. Pay attention to any insights, images, or feelings that arise—these are your intuitive messages coming through.

4. **Notice the Signs:** As you immerse yourself in the experience, be open to synchronicities or symbolic messages from the universe. These signs will often

show up in unexpected ways, helping you uncover answers to your questions.

A vision quest is a beautiful way to reconnect with your inner wisdom and invite more synchronicity into your life. It's a sacred pause, allowing you to step outside your everyday routine and receive the guidance that's waiting for you.

Creative Visualization: Bringing Your Visions to Life

Creative visualization is another powerful tool for strengthening your intuition and aligning with your highest path. By using the power of your mind's eye, you can imagine the life you desire and bring it into reality. Creative visualization works hand-in-hand with synchronicity—once you visualize your dreams, the universe begins to align events and opportunities to make them happen.

Here's a simple guide to practicing creative visualization:

1. **Find a Quiet Space:** Sit or lie down in a comfortable position. Close your eyes and take a few deep breaths to center yourself.

2. **Imagine Your Desired Outcome:** Bring to mind something you want to create or experience. It could be a new career, a fulfilling relationship, or a personal goal. Visualize it as vividly as possible—see the colors, hear the sounds, and feel the emotions of achieving it.

3. **Feel the Joy:** As you visualize, focus on the feelings of joy, gratitude, and excitement that come with realizing your vision. These emotions amplify the

power of your intention and help you align with the outcome.

4. **Release It to the Universe:** Once you've visualized your desired outcome, release it to the universe. Trust that the universe will guide you toward the steps needed to bring your vision to life. Be open to synchronicities that show up along the way—they're often the universe's way of confirming that you're on the right path.

Bonus: Free Brain Entrainment Track

To deepen your practice of creative visualization, I'm offering a free brain entrainment track designed to help you reach a state of focused relaxation and amplify your intuitive insights. Brain entrainment uses specific frequencies to synchronize your brainwaves, allowing you to tap into higher states of consciousness and creativity.

Simply listen to this track during your creative visualization sessions to enhance your focus and connection with your intuition. As you visualize your desired outcome, the brain entrainment frequencies will help you enter a state of deep relaxation, making it easier to receive intuitive guidance and manifest your vision.

* * * * *

Chapter 7 Summary: Synchronicity is one of the universe's most powerful tools for guiding you along your path. By staying open to these meaningful coincidences, you can invite more clarity, alignment, and joy into your life. Whether through a vision quest, creative visualization, or the daily practice of noticing synchronicities, you can strengthen your intuitive connection and receive the guidance you need to create the life you desire. Remember, the universe is always working with you—trust the timing and the signs.

CHAPTER 8:

"Creative Visualization: Manifesting Your Desires with Intention"

Imagine if you could consciously create the life you've always dreamed of—seeing your goals unfold exactly as you envisioned them. That's the power of creative visualization, a practice that taps into the limitless potential of your mind and allows you to manifest your desires with clarity and intention. In this chapter, we'll explore how to use creative visualization to design your life and the steps you can take to make it a daily practice.

What is Creative Visualization?

Creative visualization is the process of using your imagination to see, feel, and experience what you want to achieve as if it's already happening. It's more than just daydreaming—it's a powerful way to align your mind, body, and energy with your goals. When you focus your thoughts and emotions on what you want, you send a clear signal to the universe, inviting opportunities, resources, and synchronicities that support your vision.

The magic of creative visualization lies in its ability to engage all of your senses. You're not just thinking about what you want—you're seeing it, feeling it, hearing it, and living it in your mind. This deep sensory engagement amplifies the energy around your desires, making them more likely to manifest in your reality.

How Creative Visualization Works

At its core, creative visualization is about aligning your thoughts with the frequency of your desires. The universe operates on energy, and every thought you think carries a vibration. When you visualize your goals with clarity and positivity, you elevate your energetic frequency to match what you want to attract.

Think of it like tuning into a radio station. If you want to listen to classical music, you wouldn't tune your radio to a rock station, right? The same goes for your desires—if you want to manifest joy, abundance, or love, you need to focus your thoughts and energy on the frequency of those experiences.

The Science Behind Creative Visualization

While creative visualization has long been associated with spiritual practices, science backs up its effectiveness. Studies have shown that when we visualize an action, our brain sends the same signals as if we were actually performing that action. This means that by visualizing your goals, you're training your brain to take the necessary steps to achieve them.

Athletes, performers, and successful individuals often use visualization techniques to prepare for big moments. By mentally rehearsing their performance, they're not only building confidence but also priming their brain to execute flawlessly. The same principle applies to your personal and professional goals—visualization helps you mentally prepare and align with the outcomes you desire.

Step-by-Step Guide to Creative Visualization

Ready to start bringing your dreams to life? Here's a step-by-step guide to help you harness the power of creative visualization:

1. **Clarify Your Desire:** Before you begin, take time to get crystal clear on what you want. The more specific you are, the more powerful your visualization will be. Whether it's a new career, financial abundance, a healthier lifestyle, or a fulfilling relationship, write down your goals in detail.
2. **Find a Quiet Space:** Set aside 10-15 minutes in a quiet place where you won't be disturbed. You can sit or lie down—whatever feels most comfortable.

3. **Relax and Focus:** Close your eyes and take a few deep breaths. Let go of any tension in your body and clear your mind of distractions. Focus on your breathing and allow yourself to enter a calm, relaxed state.

4. **Engage Your Senses:** Now, begin to visualize your desire as if it's already happening. See yourself living the life you want, surrounded by the people, opportunities, and experiences you've envisioned. Engage all of your senses—what does it look, feel, smell, sound, and taste like? The more vivid your imagination, the more effective your visualization.

5. **Feel the Emotions:** As you visualize, focus on the emotions that come with achieving your goal. How does it feel to have what you desire? Are you filled with joy, excitement, peace, or gratitude? These emotions are the key to amplifying the energy around your vision.

6. **Release and Trust:** Once you've fully immersed yourself in the visualization, release it to the universe. Trust that you've set the intention, and now the universe is working to bring it to life. Let go of any need to control the outcome and stay open to the opportunities that come your way.

The Many Ways We Download Information: Clairaudience, Clairvoyance, and Beyond

Just like people have different learning styles, we also have different ways of receiving intuitive information. These intuitive "downloads" can come in many forms, and one of the most fascinating parts of the journey is discovering how *you* tune in. Here's a breakdown of the different ways people receive messages from the unseen world:

- **Clairvoyance** (Clear Seeing): This is the ability to receive information through **visions** or images. It might be a quick mental snapshot of a place, person, or event, or it could be more like a movie playing in your mind's eye. Clairvoyants often experience vivid dreams or mental pictures that hold meaning.

- **Clairaudience** (Clear Hearing): If you ever "hear" an inner voice that isn't yours—perhaps offering advice or delivering a message—you're likely experiencing clairaudience. This intuitive download involves receiving information through **sound or hearing**, whether it's literal words, music, or even a tone that signals something important.

- **Clairsentience** (Clear Feeling): This is when you intuitively know things through **feelings or physical sensations**. You might walk into a room and immediately sense the emotions of others, or feel an intuitive nudge in your body when something is off or perfectly aligned. People who are clairsentient often use terms like "gut feeling" or "vibe."

- **Claircognizance** (Clear Knowing): Have you ever just *known* something without any logical explanation? That's claircognizance, where information seems to drop into your mind fully formed, like a sudden insight or realization. It's often described as a "download" of knowledge that comes all at once.

- **Clairgustance** (Clear Tasting) and **Clairalience** (Clear Smelling): These are less common but still powerful ways to receive intuitive information. Clairgustance involves tasting something without actually eating it, while clairalience is receiving messages through scent, like the smell of a loved one's perfume when they're not physically present.

For me, as a fine arts painter and high-end residential interior designer, I see visions like I'm watching a movie. Occasionally I will have clairailience, especially when it is a salon in someone's home, where amidst the foods I'll smell pipe or cigar smoke.

SPECIAL NOTE:

Now, I have had an experience with clairaudience- I was staying with close friends at their historic mansion. It was unpleasant to say the least. It was like a bowling alley with the bouncing noise, and I had a little girl crying and mewling in my ear all night.

In the morning, after everyone had gone to work, I sat on the bed on the bed calmly putting on my make-up and explaining to the ghosts that be that I would make the white light for them, which I did.

Thankfully I had time to meditate and envision them finding peace. This Gift is not a thing that can be rushed. It is a calling, and it requires deep attention to detail, compassion and a spoonful of fearlessness with a dash of courage.

As my beloved Old Granny would say,

"It's not the dead that will hurt you,
it's the living that will get you."

Everyone has the potential to tap into one or more of these senses, and part of your intuitive journey is discovering how you naturally receive these divine downloads. You may find that you have a dominant sense, such as clairvoyance, but as you continue developing, the other "clairs" might start showing up too. Trust in your unique process—your intuition knows how to speak your language.

Increased Empathy and Compassion: The Gifts and Challenges of Being an Empath

One of the most profound gifts that often comes with heightened intuition is an increase in **empathy and**

compassion. As you open up to the energy around you, you may find that you feel more deeply—not just your own emotions, but the emotions of others as well. This expanded sensitivity can allow you to understand and connect with people in a deeper, more meaningful way. You become a mirror for their pain, joy, and experiences, which can be incredibly healing for both you and those around you.

However, this heightened empathy also comes with challenges, especially for those who identify as **empaths**. Empaths have a natural ability to absorb and feel the emotions, thoughts, and energies of others. While this can make them exceptional at offering comfort and support, it can also leave them feeling emotionally overwhelmed or drained. Without the proper boundaries and grounding practices, being an empath can feel like carrying the weight of the world.

The Dangers of Being an Empath

The danger of being an empath lies in **energetic overload**. When you constantly take on the emotional energy of others—whether it's sadness, stress, or anger—it can leave you feeling exhausted, anxious, or even physically unwell. Empaths often experience burnout if they don't establish clear boundaries or if they neglect their own self-care.

Another challenge empaths face is **emotional confusion**—the difficulty of distinguishing between their own feelings and those of the people around them. This can lead to confusion, emotional swings, and an inability to make clear decisions.

When you're constantly absorbing the emotions of others, it's easy to lose sight of your own needs and desires.

This is why **grounding** is critical. Grounding helps you stay connected to your own energy, preventing emotional overwhelm and ensuring that you're operating from a place of strength and clarity.

Grounding Practices for Empaths: Staying Centered in Your Own Energy

To thrive as an empath, it's essential to stay grounded—keeping yourself energetically rooted in your own body and in the present moment. Grounding techniques help you release any energy you've absorbed from others and re-center in your own emotional and physical space.

Here are a few **grounding practices** that are especially useful for empaths:

- **Nature Connection**: Spending time in nature is one of the easiest and most effective ways to ground yourself. Whether you're walking barefoot on the grass, gardening, or simply sitting under a tree, nature has a way of balancing your energy and calming your mind.

- **Breathwork**: Simple breathing exercises can help you ground quickly. Try the **six-second breath**—inhale for six seconds, hold for six, and exhale for six. This rhythmic breathing anchors you in your body and brings your focus back to the present moment.

- **Visualization**: Picture yourself as a tree, with roots extending from your feet deep into the earth. Imagine those roots absorbing the earth's energy, stabilizing you, and drawing out any energy you've picked up from others. This visual can quickly bring you back to your center.

- **Physical Movement**: Activities like **yoga, swimming, Qi Gong**, and walking help release stagnant energy and bring you back into your own body. These movements keep your energy flowing, preventing emotional build-up and burnout.

- **Energetic Boundaries**: Before entering a potentially draining situation, visualize a protective light or bubble around you. This energetic boundary will help prevent you from absorbing the emotions of those around you. It's a simple but powerful way to protect your energy while still engaging compassionately with others.

By incorporating these grounding practices into your daily routine, you can protect your energy and continue to develop your intuitive gifts without becoming overwhelmed. The more you ground yourself, the more empowered you'll feel to use your empathy and compassion as a force for healing—both for yourself and for those around you.

As you cultivate the practice of grounding yourself and maintaining strong energetic boundaries, you create a stable foundation from which your intuitive gifts can flourish. Once you're rooted in your own energy, it becomes easier to harness the power of your imagination and direct it with intention. This is where **creative visualization** comes into play. Grounded and centered, you're in the perfect position to use visualization not only as a tool for manifestation but as a way to deepen your connection to the intuitive wisdom within. Let's explore how creative visualization allows you to bring your inner desires into your outer reality, with clarity and confidence.

Daily Creative Visualization Practice

To maximize the effectiveness of creative visualization, consistency is key. Make it a daily practice, even if it's just for a few minutes each morning or before bed. The more you focus on your goals with clarity and intention, the more you'll notice synchronicities, inspiration, and momentum in your life.

Here are some tips for integrating creative visualization into your daily routine:

- **Morning Visualization:** Start your day with a few minutes of visualization. Before diving into your tasks, take time to mentally rehearse what you want to achieve. Visualize yourself moving through your day with ease, confidence, and joy, knowing that you're attracting the right opportunities.

- **Vision Board:** Create a vision board with images, words, and symbols that represent your desires. Place it somewhere you'll see it daily, and spend a few moments each day visualizing yourself living that reality.

- **Gratitude Visualization:** Combine gratitude with visualization by focusing on what you're thankful for while visualizing your future desires. Gratitude amplifies the positive energy around your goals and signals to the universe that you're ready to receive more.

Creative Visualization for Specific Goals

You can tailor your creative visualization practice to suit different areas of your life. Whether you're visualizing financial abundance, better health, or personal fulfillment, the process remains the same: clarity, sensory engagement, and emotional resonance.

Here are a few examples of how to use creative visualization for specific goals:

- **Career Success:** See yourself thriving in your ideal job, collaborating with amazing colleagues, and achieving the recognition and success you desire. Visualize the feeling of accomplishment and fulfillment that comes with pursuing your passion.
- **Health and Wellness:** Imagine yourself in optimal health, feeling energized, vibrant, and at peace in your body. Visualize yourself making choices that support your well-being, whether it's eating nourishing foods, exercising, or meditating.

- **Relationships:** Envision the kind of relationships you want in your life—whether romantic, family, or friendships. See yourself surrounded by love, support, and connection, and feel the joy of those meaningful relationships.

Brain Entrainment: Amplify Your Visualization

To take your creative visualization to the next level, consider investing in one of my brain entrainment albums designed to enhance your focus and relaxation during the process. Brain entrainment uses sound frequencies to synchronize your brainwaves, allowing you to access deeper states of consciousness and creativity.

Listening while you practice your creative visualization is a powerful catalyst for change. The brain entrainment frequencies will help you enter a meditative state, making it easier to visualize your desires with clarity and focus. As you listen, imagine your goals unfolding effortlessly, and trust that the universe is aligning everything to bring your vision to life.

*****

Chapter 8 Summary: Creative visualization is a powerful tool for manifesting your desires and aligning with your highest path. By using your imagination to engage your senses and emotions, you send a clear signal to the universe, amplifying the energy around your goals. Whether you're visualizing career success, health, or relationships, this practice allows you to co-create your reality with intention. With the addition of a free brain entrainment track, you can deepen your visualization experience and access the creative power within you.

CHAPTER 9:

"Breaking Through Blockages: Trusting Your Own Inner Wisdom"

As you move deeper into your intuitive journey, it's natural to encounter roadblocks—those nagging doubts, limiting beliefs, and emotional blockages that make you question your abilities. You might find yourself thinking, *"Am I really intuitive? Can I trust myself? What if I get it wrong?"* These are the moments where the real work begins. In this chapter, we'll explore how to break through these blockages, release limiting beliefs, and trust in the power of your own intuition.

The Power of Self-Trust

At the heart of intuitive development is self-trust. One of the biggest misconceptions people have is that they need someone else—a medium, a psychic, or a spiritual practitioner—to tell them what to do or see the future for them. While guidance from others can be helpful, it's important to remember that your intuition is your most reliable guide. No one can know what's best for you better than you.

The key is learning to cultivate a strong, unwavering trust in your own inner wisdom. The more you practice relying on your intuition, the clearer and more confident you'll become. In fact, the most powerful spiritual journeys come from within—not from relying on someone else's interpretation of your experiences.

Limiting Beliefs: The Biggest Blockages

Limiting beliefs are one of the most common barriers to trusting your intuition. These are the deeply ingrained thoughts and ideas that tell you you're not good enough, not intuitive enough, or that you need someone else's approval to make decisions.

Here are some common limiting beliefs that might come up as you strengthen your intuition:

- **"I'm not intuitive."** This is one of the most common beliefs people have, and it couldn't be further from the truth. Intuition isn't reserved for a select few—it's a natural ability that everyone possesses. The more you practice tuning in, the more you'll realize how intuitive you actually are.

- **"I need a practitioner to help me."** While it's true
  that practitioners can offer guidance, you don't need
  anyone else to access your intuition. In fact, relying
  too heavily on others can create dependency and
  block you from fully trusting yourself.

- **"What if I get it wrong?"** Fear of making mistakes
  is a natural part of any growth process, but intuition
  doesn't operate in the realm of right or wrong. It's
  about following what feels aligned and trusting that
  even if something doesn't go as planned, it's part of
  your learning journey.

- **"It's too hard to understand the signs."** Sometimes,
  the messages you receive from your intuition can feel
  cryptic or symbolic, leading to frustration. But
  remember, intuition often speaks through metaphor
  and imagery. Just like interpreting a dream, your
  intuitive insights require patience and practice to
  understand.

Releasing Limiting Beliefs: A Practical Approach

Breaking through limiting beliefs starts with awareness. Once
you recognize the beliefs that are holding you back, you can
begin to challenge and release them. Here's a simple exercise
to help you break free from limiting beliefs and step into your
intuitive power:

1. **Identify the Limiting Belief:** Start by writing down
   any beliefs that come up when you think about your

intuition. Is there a particular thought or fear that repeats in your mind? Write it out clearly.

2. **Challenge the Belief:** Once you've identified the limiting belief, ask yourself: *"Is this belief absolutely true? Where did it come from?"* Often, these beliefs are inherited from childhood, past experiences, or societal conditioning. By challenging them, you can begin to see how they're not based in truth.

3. **Replace with Empowering Beliefs:** After challenging the belief, replace it with a more empowering thought. For example, if your limiting belief is, *"I'm not intuitive,"* replace it with, *"I trust my intuition more each day, and it is guiding me in the right direction."* Write these empowering beliefs down and repeat them as affirmations daily.

4. **Practice Self-Validation:** Start trusting your own insights without needing external validation. When you have a gut feeling or intuitive nudge, act on it, even if it's something small. Over time, you'll build confidence in your own guidance.

You Never Need a Medium: Becoming Your Own Guide

One of the most important lessons on the intuitive path is that you never need a medium or psychic to guide you. While others can offer perspective or insight, your inner wisdom is the ultimate authority. This is especially true in deeper spiritual practices like past life regression or dream analysis, where the messages you receive are often personal and symbolic.

When I lead past life regression hypnotherapy sessions, for example, the client is always the one experiencing the feelings and visions. The practitioner's role is simply to steward the process—not to dictate, suggest, or implant ideas. The goal is for the client to discover their own insights, through their own lens, allowing them to gain deeper understanding and healing.

In the same way, you are the steward of your own intuitive journey. Whether you're analyzing a dream, working with past life memories, or receiving intuitive downloads, the messages that come through are yours to interpret. You don't need someone else to tell you what they mean—your inner wisdom already knows.

Metaphor and Symbolism: The Language of Intuition

One of the reasons people get stuck in their intuitive practice is because they expect clear, linear answers. But intuition rarely speaks in straightforward terms. Instead, it communicates through metaphor, imagery, and symbolism, much like a dream.

For example, you might have an intuitive vision of standing in front of a locked door. On the surface, this might seem like a simple image, but symbolically, it could represent a new opportunity or a part of yourself that's ready to be unlocked.

Understanding the deeper meaning requires reflection and trust in your ability to interpret these symbolic messages.

Here's how to start working with metaphor and symbolism in your intuitive practice:

1. **Notice the Imagery:** Whether you're meditating, journaling, or reflecting on a dream, pay attention to any images, symbols, or metaphors that arise. These might seem random at first, but they carry deeper meaning.

2. **Reflect on the Meaning:** Take time to reflect on the symbols. Ask yourself: *"What does this represent to me? How does it relate to my current situation or question?"* Trust your first impressions, as they are often the most accurate.

3. **Trust the Process:** Intuitive messages often unfold over time. You might not fully understand a symbol or image right away, but as you continue to work with it, its meaning will become clearer.

Definitely invest in a good dream dictionary, start a dream journal that focuses on the big takeaways. Online, I like wwwdotdreammoodsdotcom

Moving Through Blocks with Metaphor

Just as metaphor and symbolism guide us in dreams, they can also help us move through emotional or spiritual blockages. If you're feeling stuck in a particular area, try visualizing the blockage as a symbol—perhaps a wall, a locked door, or a knot in a rope. Once you have that image, imagine yourself working with it: breaking down the wall, unlocking the door, or untying the knot.

This practice allows you to bypass the conscious mind and work directly with the subconscious, where true transformation happens. By engaging with the metaphor, you're giving your intuition permission to guide you toward the solution.

* * * * *

Chapter 9 Summary: As you deepen your intuitive practice, blockages and limiting beliefs are bound to arise. The key to breaking through is learning to trust your own inner wisdom and releasing the need for external validation. Whether through past life regression, dream analysis, or everyday intuition, your guidance is always available to you. By working with metaphor and symbolism, you can navigate blockages and limiting beliefs, moving through the process with confidence and clarity. Remember, you never need a medium to access your intuition—your greatest guide is within you.

CHAPTER 10:

"Transactive Memory: The Invisible Library of Intuition"

Have you ever had a memory, scene from a movie, or a passage from a book pop into your mind at just the right moment? Maybe you were in the middle of a conversation, trying to solve a problem, or reflecting on a difficult situation, and suddenly—seemingly out of nowhere—something familiar came to you, as if offering a solution or insight.

This is **transactive memory**, the invisible yet very real library of knowledge that we all carry within us. It's a blend of remembered stories from your life, the experiences of others, and the collective wisdom of culture. It can be a scene from a movie you watched long ago, a phrase your grandmother used to say, or even a historical event that mirrors something you're going through. These memories and cultural references aren't just random—they are tools for interpreting intuitive messages and connecting with a deeper level of wisdom.

In this chapter, we'll explore how transactive memory works, how it plays a role in psychic translation, and how you can use it to better understand both your own intuition and the messages you receive when reading for others.

What is Transactive Memory?

Transactive memory refers to the shared system of storing and retrieving information across a group, culture, or even across time. It's the idea that we don't store all knowledge within ourselves but rely on the collective experiences, stories, and knowledge of others to access information when needed. It's like having an invisible mental network that you can tap into—one that connects you to past experiences, cultural references, and collective wisdom.

For example, a scene from a movie might suddenly pop into your mind while you're contemplating a decision. At first, it may seem random, but if you pause to reflect, you'll often find that this "memory" holds an important insight. Maybe it's a scene that mirrors the emotions or conflict you're facing, or it offers a symbolic message that helps you understand your next step.

In intuitive work, transactive memory becomes a powerful tool for translating psychic messages. When you receive intuitive downloads—whether through visions, feelings, or symbols—your transactive memory may kick in, offering a cultural reference or personal story that provides clarity and context.

Transactive Memory and Psychic Translation

When learning to read for yourself and others, it's important to recognize that the psychic messages you receive aren't always straightforward. They often come through in abstract, symbolic ways. This is where transactive memory plays a crucial role—it helps you translate those messages by connecting them to something familiar, whether it's a personal experience, a historical event, or a scene from a book or film.

For example, during a reading, you might receive a vision of a particular image or symbol that doesn't immediately make sense. But then, out of the blue, a story your grandmother used to tell comes to mind. This isn't a coincidence—it's your transactive memory linking the symbol to a deeper layer of meaning. The memory serves as a key to unlocking the message behind the vision.

In her past life regression hypnotherapy sessions, Callie Claire ensures that the client experiences the visions and feelings themselves, without her interference. The client's own transactive memory is what brings forward the necessary insights. The practitioner is merely a steward, guiding the process but never dictating the meaning of the imagery. This ensures that the interpretation is authentic to the client's own life and history.

Everyday Examples of Transactive Memory

Transactive memory shows up in many areas of life, not just in spiritual work. Here are a few everyday examples of how it works:

- **Family Stories:** The stories passed down through generations shape your worldview, providing insight and guidance when you need it. These stories become part of your transactive memory, offering wisdom that you can call upon when facing similar challenges.

- **Cultural References:** Films, books, music, and other forms of media become woven into the fabric of your memory. Scenes from movies or lines from songs may bubble up when you're navigating an emotional situation, offering a new way to understand what you're going through.

- **Shared Knowledge:** Your interactions with friends, family, and mentors create a collective store of knowledge. When you're stuck or confused, you might unconsciously tap into the wisdom you've absorbed from these interactions, finding solutions that are already embedded in your transactive memory.

The Story of Helen Keller: A Collective Example

A powerful example of transactive memory in action can be found in the story of Helen Keller during World War II. As described by Malcolm Gladwell in *The Bomber Mafia*, Keller, who was both blind and deaf, spoke out after the Nazi book burnings. She comforted the masses by reminding them that the knowledge contained in those books couldn't be destroyed. It had already been absorbed into the hearts and minds of the people—it was part of the collective transactive memory.

Helen Keller's words resonated deeply because she was pointing out something profound: the stories, lessons, and emotional impact of those books were already woven into the culture. They existed beyond the physical pages, living on in the collective memory of those who had read and experienced them. This is the essence of transactive memory—it preserves and shares knowledge in ways that transcend the tangible.

Using Transactive Memory in Intuitive Development

So how can you use transactive memory in your own intuitive development? Here are a few steps to help you harness this powerful tool:

1. **Trust the "Random" Thoughts:** When a memory, scene, or story pops into your mind during an intuitive reading, trust that it's not random. Pause and reflect on why this particular memory surfaced. What message might it hold? How does it connect to what you're experiencing or reading for someone else?

2. **Engage in Reflection:** After receiving intuitive messages, take time to reflect on your own transactive memory. Journal about the memories, stories, or

cultural references that came up, and see how they offer insight into the message you received.

3. **Tap Into Collective Wisdom:** When reading for others, remember that their transactive memory is just as important. Ask open-ended questions to help them tap into their own memories, stories, and experiences. This will often provide clarity and help them connect the dots in their intuitive journey.

4. **Recognize the Power of Symbols:** Just like in dream analysis, intuitive messages are often symbolic. Transactive memory helps you decode these symbols by linking them to stories, experiences, or cultural references that make sense in the current context.

Symbolism and Unexpected Imagery: Translating the Unseen

Much like dreams, intuitive messages often come in the form of metaphor and unexpected imagery. The symbols you see or feel may not make sense at first glance, but they carry layers of meaning waiting to be unlocked through transactive memory. By trusting the images and stories that surface, you can begin to interpret these messages in a way that's both personal and powerful.

For example, you might receive an image of a house during a reading. On the surface, a house could symbolize shelter or family. But if a specific memory of your childhood home comes up, it's likely that your transactive memory is offering additional insight—perhaps this is a message about safety, belonging, or returning to your roots.

Transactive Memory Through Time

Transactive memory, a system through which groups collectively store and share knowledge, mirrors the interconnected nature of dreams, the Akashic Records, and ancestral wisdom. Indigenous tribes such as the Lakota, Hopi, and Ojibwe have long recognized the power of dreams as a communal and spiritual practice, believing that dreams are not just personal experiences but a collective resource. In Lakota tradition, for instance, dreams are seen as the soul's path, guiding individuals and their communities in life and beyond. Similarly, Edgar Cayce, often called the "Sleeping Prophet," used dream states to access the Akashic Records, offering insights that transcended individual lifetimes and contributed to a shared pool of human understanding. Like the dream-sharing practices of Native American tribes, Cayce's work reflects how dreams and the Akashic Records act as transactive memory systems, connecting us to universal knowledge and shared spiritual heritage. Through these practices, individual insights become part of a greater, collective wisdom, accessible across time, space, and lifetimes.

Consider that perhaps your interest in your family tree and ancestry is fueled by a delight in your genetic story and the themes that resonate across time.

$$* * * * *$$

Chapter 10 Summary: Transactive memory is the invisible library of intuition, allowing you to access knowledge, stories, and experiences that help you translate psychic messages. Whether through family stories, cultural references, or personal memories, transactive memory weaves together past and present, offering valuable insights. By learning to trust these "random" thoughts and connections, you can better understand both your own intuitive messages and those you receive when reading for others. Remember, your intuition is always in dialogue with the collective wisdom that surrounds you.

CHAPTER 11:

"Intuition, Spirituality, and the Great Mystery"

When people talk about intuition, the conversation often drifts toward the idea of God, spirituality, or a higher power. This connection makes sense—intuition, after all, feels like a direct line to something greater than ourselves.

But what does it really mean to engage with this higher power through intuition? For some, it might mean a connection to God, while for others, it's a more abstract sense of the universe, the great Mystery, or the Creator. This chapter explores the difference between spirituality and religion, and why, when we discuss intuition, we often feel we're tapping into something divine.

Intuition and the Debate about Religion

One of the first things to acknowledge is the ongoing debate about religion and how it relates to spirituality. Many people associate intuition with a religious framework, where the messages they receive are seen as coming from a specific deity, like God in Christianity. For others, intuition is more of a spiritual practice, separate from any organized religion.

For me, intuition is deeply spiritual but not tied to a particular religion. It's like Oprah often says—my spirituality is my own personal, private practice. It's my way of connecting with the great Mystery or Creator, whatever name you choose to give that higher force. For some, it's God; for others, it's the universe, Spirit, our own Soul Self, our Ancestors or something beyond words. The name doesn't matter as much as the connection itself.

When we open ourselves to intuition, we're engaging in a dialogue with this higher power—whatever that looks like for each individual. It's a personal practice, something you can cultivate in your own way, without needing to adhere to any specific religious rules or doctrines. My best friend went to the Priest and had a conversation about this Gift, and what I can tell you is to embrace an open dialogue and become a spiritual explorer. If you feel uncomfortable, examine your boundaries and get in the Noticing-Zone. You are in control, always.

The Power of Benevolence and Prayer

One common belief is that prayer can only happen within a specific religious framework—that you can't "pray" unless you're a Christian or follow a particular faith. This idea, in my view, is petty. Prayer is not restricted to any religion. At its core, prayer is an act of benevolence in action. It's a way of asking for guidance, wishing on a star, or seeking help from your guardian angels. It's a universal practice, available to everyone.

Prayer can be as simple as taking a moment to ask for help, direction, or clarity. You don't need to follow a script or belong to a particular religion to ask for help from the divine. The intention behind your prayer is what matters. If your aim is beneficial for yourself and for the greater good, then you're aligning with the natural flow of the universe.

In my own practice, the more I serve, love, and give, the more abundance flows into my life. The more I share, the more I receive, whether it's financial wealth, love, or opportunities to make a positive impact. This alignment isn't about religious dogma—it's about living in harmony with the forces of love and generosity.

Staying in Motion: Why Action is Critical

Intuition and spirituality are deeply intertwined with action. When you feel stumped, scared, or panicked, it's easy to want to freeze, waiting for the perfect answer to appear. But in reality, staying in motion—even when you don't have all the answers—is critical to receiving intuitive guidance. It's when you're active and engaged that you serendipitously bump into the next great person, book, or idea that will help you grow and see things in a new light.

Stagnation is the enemy of intuition. If you stay stuck in one place, mentally or emotionally, it's harder for the universe to bring you the synchronicities and blessings that confirm you're on the right path. By moving forward, even when it feels uncertain, you create space for divine guidance to enter your life.

Synchronicity as Divine Confirmation

Synchronicity is one of the most powerful ways the universe communicates with us. It's those seemingly "random" coincidences that confirm you're on the right path—like a special delivery message from the divine. Maybe you're contemplating a new career direction, and suddenly you meet someone who offers you an opportunity in exactly the field you were thinking about. Or you're struggling with a decision, and a book appears that answers the very questions you've been asking.

These moments aren't accidents. They're the universe's way of saying, *"You're aligned. Keep going."* Synchronicity is a blessing, a sign that you're tuned in to your intuition and the greater flow of life. It's a form of spiritual confirmation, reminding you that you're supported, even when things feel uncertain.

When you learn to trust these synchronicities, they become a guidepost on your journey. They show up when you're in alignment with your purpose and the greater good, offering reassurance and direction when you need it most.

Being Useful and Staying Aligned with the Greater Good

There's something deeply spiritual about being useful, about serving others and contributing to the greater good. When you're in motion—whether through work, volunteering, or simply being kind and generous—you align yourself with the flow of life. You're contributing to something larger than yourself, and in doing so, you open the door to greater abundance, love, and opportunities.

This is why staying in motion, even during challenging times, is so important. It's not just about "doing" for the sake of doing—it's about staying connected to the energy of growth, movement, and service. When you're in motion, you're much more likely to encounter the synchronicities, people, and experiences that will guide you forward. And when you act from a place of love and generosity, you invite even more blessings into your life.

* * * * *

Chapter 11 Summary: Intuition often brings up conversations about God, spirituality, and religion. While many people connect their intuitive experiences with a religious framework, intuition itself is a deeply personal and spiritual practice that doesn't require adherence to any specific religion. Prayer is benevolence in action, available to everyone, regardless of faith. Staying in motion and being useful, even in times of uncertainty, is key to receiving intuitive guidance and serendipitous synchronicities. These moments of synchronicity are divine confirmations that you're aligned with your purpose and the greater good.

CHAPTER 12:

"The Path Forward:
A Review and Next Steps"

Congratulations! You've made it through a deep exploration of intuition, synchronicity, spiritual connection, and personal empowerment. By now, you've learned to trust the subtle whispers of your inner wisdom, use creative visualization to manifest your desires, and recognize the divine guidance that shows up through synchronicities. But intuition is a lifelong journey, and this chapter is designed to help you review what we've covered, anchor these lessons in your life, and set the stage for what comes next.

Lesson 1: Trusting Your Intuition

The foundation of everything we've explored is **trusting your intuition**. It's not about having all the answers right away or expecting perfection. Instead, it's about listening to your inner voice, following the subtle nudges, and trusting that even when things don't make logical sense, your intuition is leading you in the right direction.

Key Takeaway: Your intuition is always with you—ready to guide, comfort, and inspire. The more you practice listening to it and acting on it, the stronger it becomes.

Action Step: Commit to checking in with your intuition daily. Whether it's through meditation, journaling, or simply pausing to ask yourself, *"What feels right today?"*, start making this practice part of your routine.

Lesson 2: Breaking Through Limiting Beliefs

Along your intuitive journey, limiting beliefs will inevitably pop up—those doubts, fears, and thoughts that tell you you're not intuitive enough or that you need external validation. Breaking through these blockages is essential to deepening your intuitive practice.

Key Takeaway: Limiting beliefs are just stories your mind has been telling you. By recognizing them, challenging them, and replacing them with empowering thoughts, you can break free and trust your inner wisdom more fully.

Action Step: Identify one limiting belief that's been holding you back. Write it down and create an empowering statement to replace it. Repeat this new belief daily until it becomes your new reality.

Lesson 3: Synchronicity as Divine Guidance

One of the most magical parts of intuition is recognizing the **synchronicities** that show up in your life. These seemingly random coincidences are actually the universe's way of confirming that you're on the right path. They show up when you're aligned with your purpose, offering signs that you're moving in the right direction.

Key Takeaway: Synchronicity is the universe's special delivery—reminding you that you're supported and guided every step of the way. Trust these moments as divine confirmations that you're aligned with your highest good.

Action Step: Keep a **Synchronicity Journal**. Write down the synchronicities you notice each day, and reflect on how they're guiding you. This practice will help you become more attuned to the ways the universe communicates with you.

Lesson 4: Engaging with Transactive Memory

We also explored the concept of **transactive memory**—the invisible library of knowledge we carry within us. This memory consists of personal stories, cultural references, and shared experiences that offer insight when we need it most. By tapping into your transactive memory, you can better understand the psychic messages that come to you and find clarity in situations where the answers aren't immediately obvious.

Key Takeaway: Your intuition speaks through metaphor, stories, and symbols. By trusting the memories and images that pop up during your intuitive work, you can unlock deeper meaning and insight.

Action Step: The next time a memory, story, or symbol surfaces during meditation or intuitive reflection, pause and ask, *"What message does this hold for me?"* Reflect on how it might offer guidance for your current situation.

Lesson 5: Creative Visualization and Manifestation

One of the most practical tools in your intuitive toolkit is **creative visualization**. Through this practice, you've learned to harness the power of your imagination to manifest the life you desire. By seeing, feeling, and experiencing your dreams as if they're already happening, you align your energy with your goals and invite the universe to help bring them to life.

Key Takeaway: Visualization is a powerful way to create your reality. When you engage your senses and emotions in the process, you amplify the energy around your desires and accelerate their manifestation.

Action Step: Dedicate time each day to creative visualization. Whether it's five minutes in the morning or a longer session before bed, use this time to visualize your dreams and feel the emotions of achieving them.

Lesson 6: Spirituality and the Great Mystery

We also touched on the deeper, spiritual aspects of intuition— how it connects us to the great Mystery, the Creator, or whatever higher power resonates with you. Intuition is a deeply spiritual practice, allowing you to align with a greater force beyond yourself. Whether through prayer, meditation, or simply asking for guidance, you've learned that spirituality is not tied to any religion but is a personal and individual journey.

Key Takeaway: Intuition is your personal connection to the divine, the universe, or the great Mystery. It's a private, spiritual practice that doesn't require any religious framework—just your own willingness to connect and receive guidance.

Action Step: Set aside time for a **spiritual check-in** each week. Whether it's through prayer, meditation, or time in nature, use this time to reconnect with the divine in your own way. Reflect on how your intuition and spirituality are guiding you toward your purpose.

Lesson 7: Being in Motion

Finally, we discussed the importance of staying in motion. When you feel stuck or uncertain, it's tempting to freeze and wait for the perfect solution to arrive. But in reality, staying active—mentally, emotionally, and physically—allows the universe to work through you. It's in the act of moving forward, even when you're unsure, that you bump into the right people, books, or ideas that will guide you.

Key Takeaway: Being useful and staying in motion, even in the face of fear or confusion, is critical for receiving intuitive guidance and synchronicities. When you're active and engaged, you open yourself up to divine possibilities.

Action Step: The next time you feel stuck, commit to taking small, deliberate actions. Call a friend, go for a walk, or pick up a book. Trust that by staying in motion, you're creating space for the answers and synchronicities to arrive.

Your Path Forward

As you close this chapter, know that your journey with intuition is just beginning. You now have the tools to trust yourself, recognize divine guidance, and take action in alignment with your highest purpose. Remember, intuition isn't a one-time event—it's a lifelong practice of tuning in, staying open, and moving forward with confidence.

Your path forward is full of possibilities, and with each step, your intuition will continue to grow. Trust the process, honor your inner wisdom, and know that you are always supported by the universe.

* * * * *

Chapter 12 Summary: In this final chapter, we've reviewed the key lessons from your intuitive journey—trusting your intuition, breaking through limiting beliefs, recognizing synchronicities, using transactive memory, practicing creative visualization, and connecting with the divine. The path forward is about continuing these practices, staying in motion, and trusting that you are always guided by a higher power. Your intuition is a lifelong companion, and the more you engage with it, the more aligned and abundant your life will become.

* * * * *

And just in case you thought this weird journey was only happening to you and a handful of people in your own circle...

"Famous Psychic Intuitives: Learning from the Greats"

Throughout history, many well-known figures have tapped into their psychic or intuitive gifts, often surprising the world with their insights and experiences. From military generals to Hollywood stars, these individuals remind us that intuition is a universal gift available to all.

George S. Patton: One of the most unexpected psychics in history is General George S. Patton, the famous World War II commander. Patton often spoke about having vivid visions of his past lives as a soldier, believing that his tactical instincts were honed over many lifetimes of military experience. He trusted these insights to guide him through some of the most pivotal moments in his career.

Shirley MacLaine: A well-known advocate for spiritual growth, past life exploration, and psychic phenomena, actress **Shirley MacLaine** has been a trailblazer in bringing spiritual conversations into mainstream culture. In her autobiographical book *Out on a Limb*, she openly discussed her psychic experiences and belief in reincarnation, inspiring many to embrace their spiritual journeys.

Lindsay Wagner: Best known for her role as The Bionic Woman, **Lindsay Wagner** is also recognized for her deep spiritual practice and psychic abilities. She's spent decades working as a healer and advocate for emotional and spiritual well-being, helping others reconnect with their intuitive selves.

These figures, and many more like them, such as Dionne Warwick and Dolly Parton remind us that intuition transcends profession and background. Whether you're a soldier like Patton or a Hollywood star like Wagner, the power of intuition is something you can develop and rely on throughout your life.

You don't have to change careers or dive right into Healing 101, rather take all the time necessary to learn and integrate these new, and frankly life-changing gifts.

Protecting Your Energy and Staying Grounded: Stay Zen, Set Boundaries, and Keep It Fun

As you embark on your intuitive journey, there's one golden rule to keep in mind: *Protect your energy like it's the last piece of chocolate in the box!*

Developing your intuition is exciting, but it doesn't mean you have to be wide open to all the energies swirling around. Think of your intuition as a delicate instrument—it works best when tuned properly, with healthy boundaries and a solid grounding routine.

Remember, even the most famous psychics knew the importance of setting boundaries. Whether you're connecting with people, places, or spiritual realms, think of your **energetic boundaries** as your personal bubble—a force field that keeps the good vibes in and the not-so-great stuff out.

You can still be kind, connected, and compassionate without getting overwhelmed. It's like wearing a fabulous outfit and adding a cute umbrella when it starts to rain—still you, but with extra protection!

And let's not forget the fun part—**grounding yourself!** Whether it's doing yoga in your living room, getting your hands dirty in the garden, or taking a stroll to clear your head, staying grounded can be a playful, nurturing practice. Think of it as a way to recharge your batteries—maybe even with a bit of whimsy! Need a quick energy reset? Pop in some Qi Gong moves or a six-second breath. Picture it as pressing the "refresh" button for your spirit.

At the end of the day, keeping your energy protected and your boundaries strong will help you move through your intuitive journey with confidence and ease. And the more fun you have with it, the more aligned you'll be. So, create your sacred space, keep your vibes high, and remember: Your intuition is a gift that thrives when you're feeling your best— calm, centered, and maybe even laughing along the way.

Your Journey Ahead: Keep Trusting, Keep Exploring

As you complete this book, remember that your intuition is a journey, not a destination. You've learned how to listen to your inner wisdom, recognize synchronicities, and explore the unseen world through practical tools like creative visualization and grounding techniques. But this is only the beginning.

The more you practice, the more your intuition will grow. Keep asking questions, keep exploring, and most importantly, keep trusting yourself. As you continue on your path, you can deepen your practice by:

- Exploring new spiritual tools, like brain entrainment or guided meditations
- Joining my community of like-minded people for support and online learning
- Staying curious and open to new experiences, people, and teachings that come your way

Your intuition is a lifelong companion, ready to guide you whenever you need it. Stay connected to it, and let it lead you into a life that's aligned with your highest self.

In the meantime, Stay Zen, Set Boundaries, and Keep It Fun!!!

Callie XO

Give, Serve, Love!!!

Prayer Preparation and Ancestral Guidance

Prayer, especially during challenging times, often requires a process of grounding and preparation. For me, that begins with a simple physical practice: rolling my shoulders forward and back, syncing my breath with the movement. I inhale as my shoulders rise, expanding the space in my chest, and exhale as I roll them back, releasing tension. This mindful movement opens my body and calms my mind, helping me enter a state of prayerful presence.

As I continue, I focus on areas of tightness, gently massaging my neck, jaw, and face to further relax. Sometimes, when I'm alone, I sing a round robin of "hallelujah," allowing the melody to flow, bringing me into a deeper state of peace. Once I feel centered and open, I ask my ancestors in heaven for guidance. I invite them to direct me toward the answers that reflect the higher good, trusting that they are helping me navigate toward clarity and wisdom from a place of divine connection. This practice becomes a way of bridging the physical and spiritual, inviting peace and insight into the moment.

Give yourself grace to experiment with different ways of meditating in nature. Maybe you have health issues but you really want to go hiking- so find a buddy and go quite hiking. The new trend of introverts gathering together to read in silence is so reassuring and companionable.

My message is to always Keep Going! Find a way to amend the 'no'.

This is why the **"Keep Calm and Carry On"** motto resonates with me because it captures the determination, grit, and humor that kept the WWII generation moving forward— even when everything seemed uncertain. That same energy is what I want to bring into *Unlock Your Inner Magic*. This mindset reminds us that sometimes the most powerful intuition comes when we trust ourselves in the face of adversity, stay grounded, and tap into our creative problem-solving—just like they did on the WWII homefront.

And for a fun bonus, here's a lively reading list to inspire all of us, with a mix of adventure, resilience, and a dash of witty banter:

- **The Good Shepherd** by C.S. Forester (*Greyhound*, anyone?): Follow a no-nonsense naval commander as he navigates the wilds of the Atlantic in this thrilling WWII sea story. You'll be on the edge of your seat— and maybe unlock some leadership intuition along the way.

- **The Accidental President:** Harry Truman's story of being thrown into the highest office during the final days of the war is all about trusting in yourself, even when you didn't see the challenge coming. Perfect for an intuitive nudge of confidence.

- **Haven** by Ruth Gruber: A tale of hope, empathy, and courage, Ruth Gruber's efforts to rescue Jewish refugees is a testament to following one's heart and instincts—something we can all channel in our daily lives.

- **The Hiding Place** by Corrie Ten Boom: When it comes to perseverance and forgiveness, Corrie's story is unmatched. This moving memoir helps us remember that intuition and faith can guide us even in the darkest times.

- **Mrs. Ike** by Susan Eisenhower Learn how the women behind the scenes made just as much impact on victory with grace, wit, and an intuitive flair that still inspires today.

- **D.E. Stevenson's Mrs. Tim Carries On:** This delightfully funny WWII novel brings charm and wit to wartime, reminding us that a sense of humor is essential when keeping calm (and maybe a little chocolate too).

These stories from WWII, filled with incredible bravery, resilience, and humor, serve as a reminder that we all have the power to unlock our own intuition and inner strength—sometimes, we just need a little nudge from history!

Keeping in motion allows us to haphazardly allow the Universe, the divine to bump us into the next big idea, the next big person, career move, and passion project.

You are loved, and loveable. Always.

Keep Calm and Carry On!

Callie XO